JOHN PENNINGTON

Telephone Sales Excellence

Better connections for easier sales results

ACCELA

Telephone Sales Excellence
© 2019 John Pennington

An Accela Book

Accela is an Australian owned company that specialises in high impact sales performance improvement. We're passionate about helping people to be their best and to achieve their sales goals. What differentiates Accela is our commitment to people first and foremost by helping them leverage a treasure trove of resources to easily solve their challenges.

Accela was founded by John Pennington, a sales executive with over 20 years' sales excellence with blue chip Australian and international organisations. For more information about how Accela can boost your sales performance:

+61 (02) 9368 7969
info@accela.com.au
www.accela.com.au

ACCELA

Table of Contents

"Never go backward. Attempt, and do it with all your might. Determination is power."

Charles Simmons

1. Opening

Desired result:

To put the customer in a positive, receptive frame of mind and gain permission to ask questions.

Voice Flexibilty

"Words are, of course, the most powerful drug used by mankind." Rudyard Kipling

Your Voice in Selling

It's a funny thing when we think about how much time we spend "looking good". We all choose what we want to wear or shave. We spend time on things like make-up and hair styles. Some of us spend a significant time reading fashion sites and doing retail therapy. So then, when we spend so much of our time at work on the phone, it begs the question: How much effort do we spend on "sounding good"? Even when our work depends upon how we sound, we often spend more time "looking good" than "sounding good"! You should use your vocal flexibility to help you create receptive buyers.

"Sounding Good" Practice

Read aloud the following paragraph in your "natural" manner:

"Practise as many different tones and speeds as you can. See how many different 'voices' you can create. Be warned, though: if you do not practise, all voices different from yours will feel uncomfortable. This is not a good basis for judging. Practise, and then try some new tones or speeds that you can add to your calls."

Now, read it aloud again:
- with a higher pitched voice
- with a lower voice
- more quickly
- more slowly
- as if you were very bored
- as if it was the most exciting news you had ever heard
- as if you were Michael Jackson
- as if you were Austin Powers
- as if you were Darth Vader.

Continue this exercise, using as many different 'voices' as you can. Be an actor; see how flexible you can be!

"Sounding Good" by How You Say It

1. Make sure you're pronouncing every consonant, focusing on the endings of words.

2. Open your mouth a little wider.

3. Smile as you speak.

4. Practise before you get on the phone by doing a little warm-up.

5. Treat the 10th call like the first call. Assume your next call could be your best opportunity ever.

"Sounding Good" by What You Say

1. Highlight a word or idea in every sentence.

2. Eliminate wasted words and noises: "uhhhhh", "ummm", "but", "you know", "actually".

3. Use a pause, instead of "ummms", after an important point and before an important point.

4. Avoid jargon.

5. Talk about what you can do, not what you can't do.

6. Use "story selling" by painting pictures with your words.

7. Be specific. (Approximates will reduce your credibility.)

8. Your body language affects how you sound, so keep it positive.

✓ Self-Assessment
Rate Yourself on the Following:

How urgently do you need to work on this?
Rank yourself below for both ease and impact.

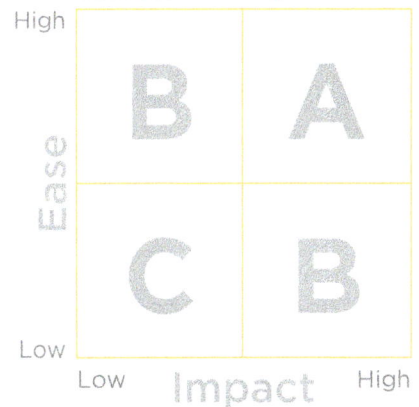

1. How much voice flexibility do you have?

   ☹ 1   2   3   4   5   6 ☺

2. How well do you practise sounding good?

   ☹ 1   2   3   4   5   6 ☺

3. What is your motivation to improve?

   ☹ 1   2   3   4   5   6 ☺

High

Ease

B	A
C	B

Low

Low   Impact   High

A = Start today | B = This week
C = After all A & B

Notes

_____

_____

_____

_____

_____

Open to Win

"Wise men speak because they have something to say. Fools speak because they have to say something." Plato

Winning Attitude

Because a winning attitude starts with your approach to prospects and customers, be sure to have genuine concern and interest in their situation.

Don't fall into the trap of starting the day thinking, "I'm going to sell to a lot of people today." Instead, say to yourself, "I'm going to help people by actively listening to what they tell me, building rapport with them, asking great questions and presenting how our services are of value."

Winning Image

Before you even make the call, you start creating interest through your attitude and state of mind. You must have a clear objective that you hope to achieve from the call. Understand your market – what are they generally trying to accomplish and what issues they generally might face. You are then in the right frame of mind.

Sounding like a radio announcer will not guarantee interest, so it is important to ensure you sound confident, competent, professional and friendly, without going over the top.

Know your call process and be able to skilfully step through each stage. This is a sure-fire way to show your buyer that you are worth talking to.

Winning with Call Screeners

If an assistant or secretary picks up the phone when you are trying to reach the decision maker, that person becomes the most important person at that moment and you should treat him/her as such. You must be prepared to work through the ranks and sell to each person as you progress to the main decision maker. By understanding their role as a protector of the buyer's time, you can be prepared to help them do their job by communicating a clear and worthy reason for the call. If you are not prepared with this vital piece of information when asked, "What is this in reference to?" you fail the first test and become another person just "selling something".

Use these strategies to win over screeners

1. Help the screener understand that you have ideas of value that can potentially help the decision maker.

2. Ask them for help. This will empower them to work with you.

3. Prepare a strategy for dealing with screeners. Know the answer before they ask the question.

4. Collect information. Prepare questions for the screener that will help you gain information that you can use to customise your conversation with the decision maker.

5. Be confident and positive in your tone of voice.

6. Have a powerful justification ready. Highlight the relevance and benefit of your call to the buyer.

TIP

Do's and Don'ts
Don't ask, "Who is the person that looks after ..." Instead say, "I'm looking for the name of the person who looks after ..."

Self-Assessment
Rate Yourself on the Following:

How urgently do you need to work on this?
Rank yourself below for both ease and impact.

1. How much of a winning attitude do you have?

   ☹ 1   2   3   4   5   6   ☺

2. How well do you work with screeners?

   ☹ 1   2   3   4   5   6   ☺

3. How well do you prepare for call screening?

   ☹ 1   2   3   4   5   6   ☺

	High		
Ease	B	A	
	C	B	
Low			
	Low	Impact	High

A = Start today | B = This week
C = After all A & B

Notes

_____

_____

_____

_____

_____

_____

_____

_____

Opening Structure

"Your big opportunity may be right where you are now." Napoleon Hill

In the Beginning

Long before you first pick up the phone, you need to ensure your mind is right – that you have the right attitude. Be sure that you value what you are selling and that you value the thoughts and ideas of those to whom you are selling. Try to understand what is important to the people you are about to call, what they want and need, and how can you help them achieve their goals. Then work on a standard opening structure.

Spark Interest

Please complete the standard structure below with what is relevant to your situation.

You: "Good morning, _____, I'm John with company XWZ. I'm calling today because depending upon what you're doing in the area of ... A ... there's a chance we might be able to help you ... B ... your ... C. If now is a good time, I'd like to ... D ... your situation and see if this is something you would like to ... E.

Your options:

A. Product/service area

B. Save, consolidate, cut down on, reduce, free up, lessen, soften, slice, etc.

C. Costs, annoyance, waste, burden, bother, hassle, etc.

D. Discuss, ask some questions about, go over, review, look into your

E. Consider, review, arrange a meeting about, know more about.

Avoid anything that can turn off a prospect such as:

1. "I was wondering if you had made a decision yet?" This is too easy to say no to.

2. "I thought I would just check in with you." This is lazy since it offers them nothing.

3. "Just touching base again." See above.

4. "You haven't placed an order for some time, why is that?" This is both lazy and negative.

5. "It's John from ABC and I wanted to see if you were interested in our products" This is salesy and offers no benefit.

6. "Did you receive the email I sent?" This adds no value; what does it prove either way?

7. "I'm your new account manager and I wanted to introduce myself." Lazy and no benefit.

Self-Assessment
Rate Yourself on the Following:

How urgently do you need to work on this?
Rank yourself below for both ease and impact.

1. How natural is your opening statement?

   ☹ 1 2 3 4 5 6 ☺

2. How well can you create various opening statements?

   ☹ 1 2 3 4 5 6 ☺

3. What is your ability to perform a great opening every time?

   ☹ 1 2 3 4 5 6 ☺

High

Ease

B	A
C	B

Low

Low   Impact   High

A = Start today | B = This week
C = After all A & B

Notes

_____

_____

_____

_____

_____

_____

_____

_____

_____

Motivating Questions

"Questions show you care!" Anonymous

Ask First

To be successful in sales you must ask questions, but not just any question will do. Keep in mind that before you start asking questions, you must gain the client's permission to do this. You must also give them a good reason to participate in this discussion. Only questions that motivate the client to "want to" respond will produce positive outcomes.

Motivating questions will help you get your clients in the "yes" mindset that will accelerate your sales process.

Motivating question example:
- "Would you mind answering a few questions so that I can focus on what is most important to you?"

By pulling this sentence apart we can identify the crucial elements:
- "Would you mind answering a few questions" – gains permission to ask questions
- "... so that I can focus on what is most important to you?" – provides benefit

The desired effect is achieved:

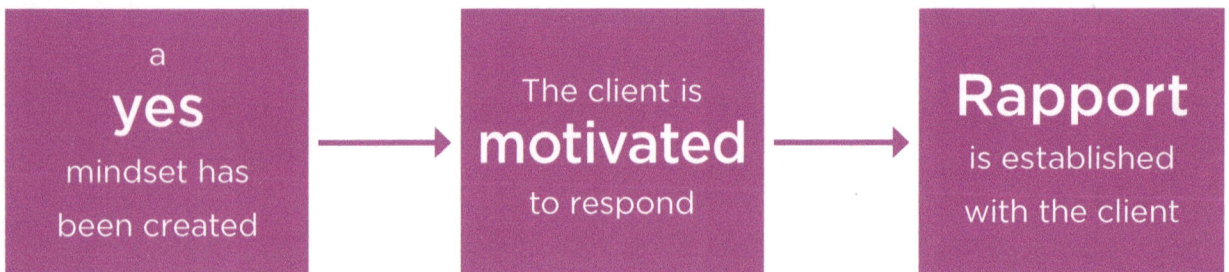

a **yes** mindset has been created	→	The client is **motivated** to respond	→	**Rapport** is established with the client

Self-Assessment
Rate Yourself on the Following:

1. How well do you understand what a motivating question is?

   ☹   1   2   3   4   5   6   ☺

2. How often do you use a motivating question?

   ☹   1   2   3   4   5   6   ☺

3. How effective are your motivating questions?

   ☹   1   2   3   4   5   6   ☺

How urgently do you need to work on this?
Rank yourself below for both ease and impact.

High

Ease

B	A
C	B

Low

Low   Impact   High

A = Start today | B = This week
C = After all A & B

Notes

_____

_____

_____

_____

_____

_____

_____

_____

_____

"The most important trip you may take in life is meeting people halfway."

Henry Boyle

2. Gathering Requirements

Desired result:

To gather, uncover, clarify and develop client requirements for your presentation and to build rapport.

Funnel Questioning

"If you don't take care of the customer, somebody else will." Stanley Marcus

A conversation flows just like a waterfall and a good salesperson can easily learn to direct it so that it produces the most useful information. If you imagine that the water flows firstly from an initial approach by a salesperson that sets the scene for the conversation to flow. Then it flows through a series of funnels that follow the same pattern. Each starts by welcoming a wide ranging response, from this probing that narrows down the information to clarify and affirm problems or desires and then specific. Finally confirmation is sort to ensure that you have everything correct. Throughout this flow of funnels you are collecting information that you can use in the later sales step of presenting. The better you collect this information the more powerful and persuasive you can make your presentation.

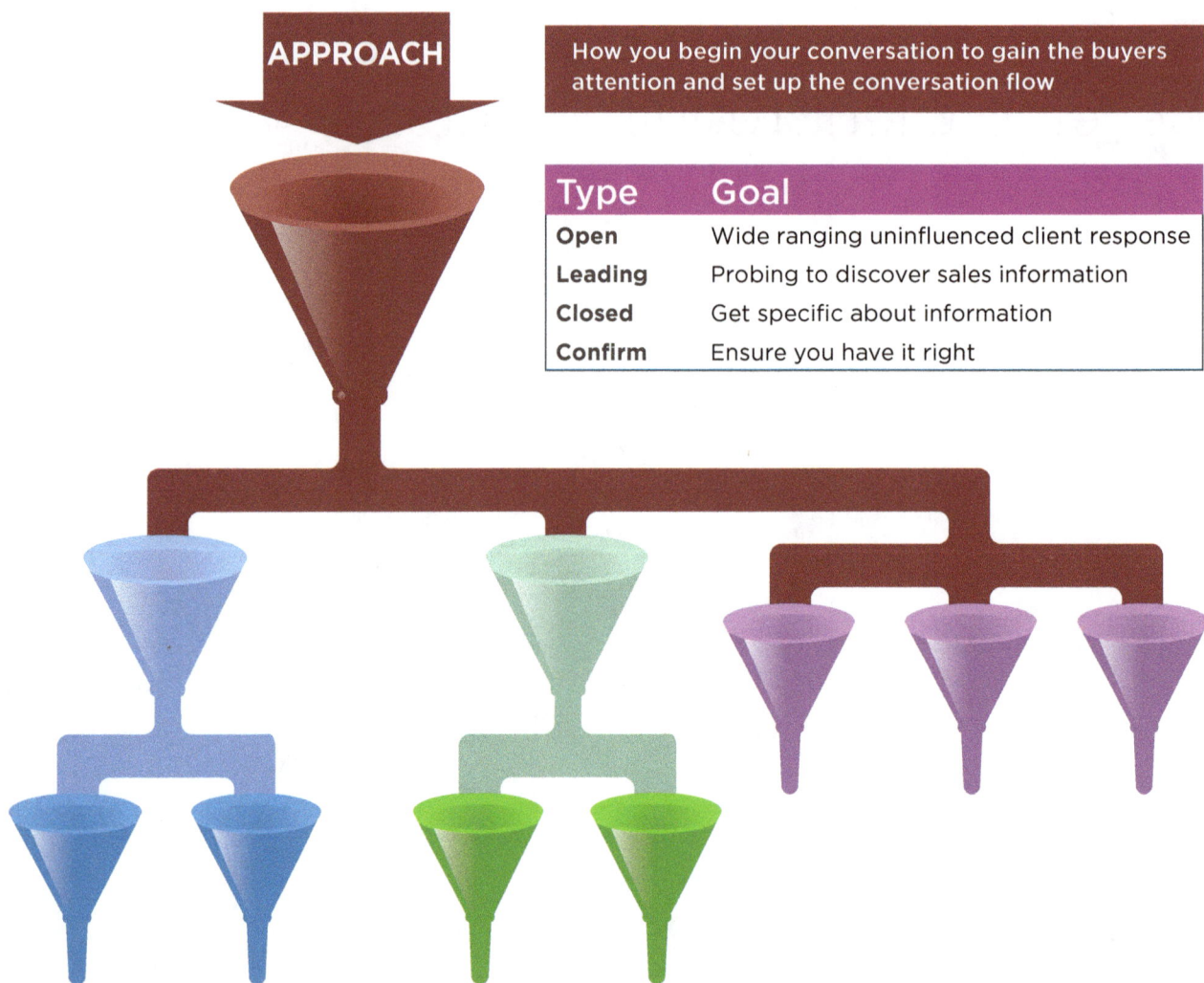

APPROACH

How you begin your conversation to gain the buyers attention and set up the conversation flow

Type	Goal
Open	Wide ranging uninfluenced client response
Leading	Probing to discover sales information
Closed	Get specific about information
Confirm	Ensure you have it right

✓ Self-Assessment
Rate Yourself on the Following:

1. How well do you understand the difference between the main types of questions?

   ☹ 1   2   3   4   5   6 ☺

2. How efficiently do you utilise each type of question?

   ☹ 1   2   3   4   5   6 ☺

3. What is your awareness of your questioning skill gaps?

   ☹ 1   2   3   4   5   6 ☺

How urgently do you need to work on this?
Rank yourself below for both ease and impact.

High	B	A
Ease	C	B
Low		

Low   Impact   High

A = Start today | B = This week
C = After all A & B

Notes

_____

_____

_____

_____

_____

_____

_____

_____

_____

_____

_____

From Open to Leading

"By failing to prepare, you are preparing to fail." Benjamin Franklin

Understanding the Difference

Depending on the type of questions you ask your client, you will receive either influenced or uninfluenced responses. Open questions tend to generate longer, uninfluenced answers that allow you to begin to understand what's important to the client. Although they're still classified as open questions, leading questions influence clients' responses around specific areas.

Open and leading questions will skyrocket your sales, as they are the key to unlocking each and every client's unique requirements. Below are some examples to get you going.

If you're looking for long lasting benefits invest time in perfecting these simple yet powerful question types.

The example below I learnt from my good friend and sales guru Nikki Owen where she illustrates the ideal combination of using open, leading and closed questions to pinpoint a customer's specific requirements:

Sales person: *"What's important to you?"* (Open question)

Customer: *"Price, quality and efficiency."* (Uninfluenced response)

Sales person: *"Why is price important to you?"* (Leading question based on price)

Customer: *"So I can be more competitive in winning new business."* (Influenced response based on price related question)

Sales person: *"If I can demonstrate how we can help you win more business, will you review our proposition?"* (Closed question to gain agreement)

Customer: *"Yes"* (influenced, definite response)

This process can be repeated easily over and over in any sales conversation the idea is to focus on what the customers believes is important and then developing this towards an action.

We ask questions because:

1. People believe what *they* say much more than what *we* tell them.

2. Objections are created by salespeople talking too much.

3. People will reject what salespeople say but not what *they* say.

Important rules to follow

1. Listen to the buyer's answer and relate your next question to it. Don't mindlessly follow a list of questions.

2. Aim to uncover their problems or needs so that when you present they will pay more attention.

3. Don't make it an interrogation.

4. Aim to move their thinking towards a better understanding of their problem or desire.

Self-Assessment
Rate Yourself on the Following:

How urgently do you need to work on this?
Rank yourself below for both ease and impact.

1. How comfortable are you with using open questions?

☹ 1 2 3 4 5 6 ☺

2. How comfortable are you with using leading questions?

☹ 1 2 3 4 5 6 ☺

3. How would you evaluate your use of open and leading questions in every sales call?

☹ 1 2 3 4 5 6 ☺

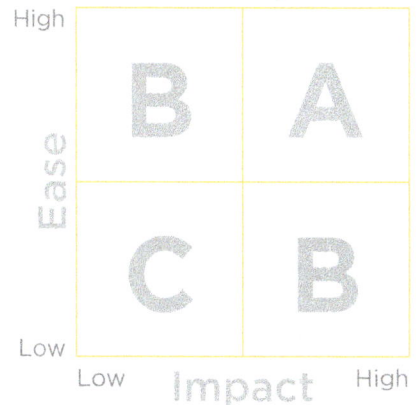

A = Start today | B = This week
C = After all A & B

Notes

_____

_____

_____

_____

Sales Questions

"Become genuinely interested in other people – ask questions." Dale Carnegie

In the Beginning

In truth, most salespeople can gather basic background facts. However, the oustanding salesperson ignites the thinking and emotions of buyers and uncovers what will spur them to take action. Use the question categories and questions below to do this with your buyers.

Warm-up Questions

- Have your responsibilities and needs evolved since you started with the company?
- What would you say you like most about your work?
- What would you say is different about your organisation's needs today from when you started?
- What are your most pressing issues?
- Many organisations/people use x and y. Can I ask if this is the case with you?

Qualifying Questions

- Can I ask you what prompted your interest in this product/service?
- How much are you going to spend on your product/service this year?
- How important is this product/service to your organisation?
- What do you expect from a supplier?
- What contracts currently exist with suppliers?

Thought-Provoking Questions

- What would you like to see happen in the future?
- What do you hope to accomplish?
- What needs are not currently being met?
- Is this important enough for you to devote a few minutes to exploring some solutions?
- What if I could give you the same/better/similar solution for a lower price?

To-Build-Up-Concern Questions

- Are you able to devote sufficient time to other projects while dealing with this problem?
- Is that also leading to higher costs for you?
- What do you see as the potential impact on you?
- Who else is affected by that?
- How important is that?
- What are the implications of that?

Finding-Out-Where-You-Stand Questions

- How are we looking on that proposal?
- Are you happy with what we have provided so far?
- So ... what do you think?
- Is there anything that would prevent you from moving forward on this proposal?
- Is it just me, or is something bothering you about this proposal?

Self-Assessment
Rate Yourself on the Following:

1. How well do you ask questions?

   ☹ 1 2 3 4 5 6 ☺

2. How well can you ask different types of questions?

   ☹ 1 2 3 4 5 6 ☺

3. What is your ability to gather what is important to the sale?

   ☹ 1 2 3 4 5 6 ☺

How urgently do you need to work on this?
Rank yourself below for both ease and impact.

	High		
Ease	B	A	
	C	B	Low
	Low	Impact	High

A = Start today | B = This week
C = After all A & B

Notes

_____

_____

_____

_____

_____

_____

_____

_____

_____

_____

_____

"Internalise the Golden Rule of sales that says, 'All things being equal, people will do business with, and refer business to, those people they know, like, and trust.'"

Bob Burg

3. Presenting

Desired result:

To conduct a persuasive, interactive presentation based upon what the client told you in your questioning.

Transition to Presentation

"People buy benefits not features – air bags are boring, protecting the lives of your family is riveting!" Anonymous

The Secret

The secret to a persuasive sales presentation is to present only what people are interested in, based upon what they told you in your questioning.

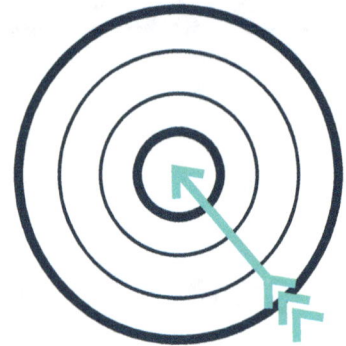

Present with Power

1. **Transition from your questioning**
   Let them know you are finished questioning, and spark their interest again:
   "Samantha, based upon what you've told me I am sure we can help you particularly around your need for (insert biggest benefit to this client)"

2. **Paraphrase your understanding**
   Eloquently rephrase in your persuasive and lightly embellished way the needs, concerns and desires they just related to you:
   "Let's review what we've covered so far"
   Need/concern/desire 1
   Need/concern/desire 2
   Need/concern/desire 3
   Does that sound like what you are looking for?"

3. **Clearly explain what they will get**
   Only talk about what they told you they are interested in especially, in terms of what the results they will receive:
   "Luke by having product/service 1 it will allow you to result 1, also product/service 2 will enable you to result 2"

Further Presentation Tips

1. People buy results. Concentrate on the results you deliver.

2. Prepare sensory descriptions of your results. Think about how your results are seen, heard, and felt, both physically and emotionally. Help them experience the results in advance.

3. Number your points as you present them. This will increase their impact, help the buyer to follow you, and reinforce the benefits.

4. Provide proof. Testimonials or case studies may be used but they must be approved, referenced and recent.

5. Use specific numbers. Round numbers are questioned more. People believe more research has gone into precise numbers, whereas round numbers are thought to be "pulled out of the air".

6. Create urgency. Use expiry dates, special offers, limited time specials, etc.

Self-Assessment
Rate Yourself on the Following:

How urgently do you need to work on this?
Rank yourself below for both ease and impact.

1. How well do you transition to presentation?

☹ 1   2   3   4   5   6   ☺

2. How well do you link benefits to client information gathered?

☹ 1   2   3   4   5   6   ☺

3. Present the results of what your product/service can do?

☹ 1   2   3   4   5   6   ☺

High

Ease

	B	A
	C	B

Low

Low   Impact   High

A = Start today | B = This week
C = After all A & B

Notes

_____

_____

_____

_____

_____

_____

_____

_____

_____

_____

Present Yourself in a Controlled Manner

"The most important thing is to remember that if rapport gets broken, you re-establish it quickly, whatever it takes." Richard Bandler

Buying You First

People buy you first, and then they buy the product you are selling. Clients rarely differentiate products or services; the real difference is in who is doing the selling. You sell yourself first.

Control, or presence, is the level of confidence that you project to others, which ultimately affects how they see you. Most people think of control as something that you can only "see", such as stage presence, but bear in mind that your voice can have as much control as your presence itself. Control creates a feeling whereby your client will feel they can depend on you. This will lead to enhanced rapport; it will add to your sales strength and help to create positive energy between your client's needs and your business.

TIP **You can create voice control through:**
• tone • speed of talking • articulation • confidence • quick thinking • wit

---

Control requires special effort during sales calls as your client will not be able to see you, so sustaining interest and enthusiasm can be challenging. You can emphasise your control in the following ways:

1. Always be dynamic, no matter how many phone calls you have made that day.

2. Keep your pace in check. Excessive rushing can indicate nervousness or inexperience, and slowness can indicate boredom.

3. Emphasise "neon" words – words that your client has used that seem to "light up" the sentence.

4. Change the tone of your voice throughout the conversation to convey interest.

5. Keep your voice positive. Any kind of annoyance or exasperation will kill any previous rapport you may have had, and it will all but eliminate any chance of building rapport in the first place.

6. Try to smile or sit up in your chair. This will create energy and will make your voice more positive. If your voice doesn't contain a positive attitude, it will work against you in selling.

7. Use positive descriptive words such as "brilliant" and "powerful".

8. Remain polite at all times. Avoid slang, over-familiarity, and bad manners (such as sighing, yawning, chewing).

9. Continually refer to their name, the name of their organisation, and the name of your organisation.

Self-Assessment
Rate Yourself on the Following:

How urgently do you need to work on this? Rank yourself below for both ease and impact.

1. How well do you stay dynamic?

   ☹ 1   2   3   4   5   6   ☺

2. How well do you keep pace and tone?

   ☹ 1   2   3   4   5   6   ☺

3. How well do you use "neon" words?

   ☹ 1   2   3   4   5   6   ☺

High

Ease

B   A

C   B

Low

Low   High
Impact

A = Start today | B = This week
C = After all A & B

Notes

_____

_____

_____

_____

_____

_____

_____

_____

Absolutely FABulous

"No one can long make a profit producing anything unless the customer makes a profit using it." Samuel Pettingill

Staying Relevant

Red, round, large, sweet. Your first thought after reading those four words was probably, "So what?" That's precisely what goes through a customer's mind when they're presented with a product's or service's features as a solution to their problems. Avoid being a "features victim" by using this FAB selling technique.

By applying the FAB (Feature, Advantage, and Benefit) technique, salespeople can relate a product/service's benefits to customer's needs.Why? Because people buy benefits, not features.

Explanation	Example	The real deal
Feature		
A feature is a physical characteristic of a product/service.	"The car includes a pre-installed GPS system".	Physical characteristics alone have very little persuasive power because customers are interested in purchasing benefits that meet their needs, not features.
Advantages		
An advantage explains why a feature is useful and how it can help the customer.	"Pre-installed GPS means that it's easier to use and you will never loose your way by running out of battery".	Clients want to know why your product or service is better than the competition's and why they should buy it. The key is to apply your knowledge of your products/services and align it to your customer's needs so that they can see how those advantages directly benefit them.
Benefits		
A benefit refers to the advantage the product/service brings to the client's stated requirements.	"You said that you were worried your hand held GPS could get stolen, that you often forgot it and that it was a hassle to charge. Well with the pre-installed GPS you will never have to worry about these again; stress free navigation."	Clients want to answer the question "What's in it for me?" Your responsibility during the presentation is to highlight how your product/service will solve their specific problems or meet their specific needs.

Self-Assessment
Rate Yourself on the Following:

1. Rate your understanding of the FAB technique.

   ☹ 1   2   3   4   5   6   ☺

2. What is your ability to differentiate between a feature and a benefit?

   ☹ 1   2   3   4   5   6   ☺

3. How well do you emphasise benefits during your presentation?

   ☹ 1   2   3   4   5   6   ☺

How urgently do you need to work on this?
Rank yourself below for both ease and impact.

High	B	A
Ease	C	B
Low		

Low   Impact   High

A = Start today | B = This week
C = After all A & B

Notes

_____

_____

_____

_____

_____

_____

_____

_____

_____

_____

"Become genuinely interested in other people – ask questions."

Dale Carnegie

4. Handling Objections and Closing

Desired result:

To easily overcome objections and close using a commitment for action that moves the client closer to the sale.

Objection-Handling Essence

"Every adversity carries with it the seed of an equivalent or greater benefit."
Anonymous

Keeping Focus

One of the factors that separates successful salespeople from everyone else is that they always keep their eye on the ball. In a sales scenario this translates into building the kind of relationship the buyer wants and selling the buyer real value. The attitudes listed below will help you stay focused and make it easier for you to uncover objections.

- Attitude 1: Be open and use all your resources and knowledge to uncover your buyer's objections.

- Attitude 2: Welcome objections; always be positive and sincere, and refrain from arguing or contradicting.

- Attitude 3: Acknowledge and handle a buyer's objections with sensitivity.

- Attitude 4: Be empathetic. Although an objection may seem unfounded to you, it's still real for the buyer.

- Attitude 5: In order to gain their trust, treat the buyer as a friend and build a strong relationship which will make them feel comfortable about raising objections.

- Attitude 6: There's always the tendency to prove to the buyer that you're right and they are wrong, but this negative attitude will only cause discomfort in the relationship.

- Attitude 7: Always remember that objections present sales opportunities since they are the gateway into the buyer's mind; they are the basis on which true partnering relationships are built.

TIP **To be able to reap the benefits of objections you must make the buyer believe you are truly grateful that they raised their concern. Be sure to just empathise with their concern and not agree to their actual objection. Saying some of the following remarks will help you project a positive attitude:**

1. "I completely understand what you're saying. I'd probably be concerned about the same thing."

2. "If I were purchasing this package, I'd probably be asking the same questions."

3. "You're absolutely right, Mr. Smith, and I understand your dilemma."

Self-Assessment
Rate Yourself on the Following:

How urgently do you need to work on this? Rank yourself below for both ease and impact.

1. What is your skill at uncovering objections during a sale?

   ☹ 1   2   3   4   5   6   ☺

2. Rate your ability to act as a counsellor/adviser to gain the buyer's trust.

   ☹ 1   2   3   4   5   6   ☺

3. How often do you respond positively when a buyer raises an objection?

   ☹ 1   2   3   4   5   6   ☺

High

Ease

Low

B	A
C	B

Low   Impact   High

A = Start today | B = This week
C = After all A & B

Notes

_____

_____

_____

_____

_____

_____

_____

_____

_____

_____

Objection-Handling Process

"Selling is the art of solving problems through patiently asking questions and listening." Michael Oliver

Ride the Wave

The purpose of a sales objection is to throw you off course, but what would happen if instead of fighting the wave you just went with the flow?

This six-step objection-handling process will have you riding the sales wave in no time.

1. Anticipate objections

As many as 80% of objections are recurrent, so being prepared for those will give you the confidence and motivation you need to handle that unknown 20%. Also, remember to always structure your presentations to show your product/service in the best light.

2. Show you care

Relax, actively listen, and remain in rapport. Don't jump in with an answer. This is the first time the buyer has raised the issue, so treat it as if it were the first time you've heard it as well.

3. Assess the objection

1. Is it an impossible objection to overcome?
2. Is it a request for more information?
3. Is it a condition for a sale?
4. Is it a minor or a major objection?

4. Clarify the objection

Make sure you understand the objection and trial close to uncover any hidden objections.

5. Overcome the objection

Select a technique that will give you the best chance to overcome the objection. Also, remember to make sure the client confirms that the objection has been resolved.

6. Trial close

Handle another objection or close the sale.

TIP

Rapport Through Humour:
Humour is a great way to help overcome objections if you're in rapport and/or if the situation is right.

Self-Assessment
Rate Yourself on the Following:

How urgently do you need to work on this? Rank yourself below for both ease and impact.

1. Rate your ability to anticipate objections.

   ☹ 1 2 3 4 5 6 ☺

2. Do you "jump the gun" and try and come up with an answer even before the buyer has finished expressing their thoughts?

   ☹ 1 2 3 4 5 6 ☺

3. How effectively do you use trial closing to overcome objections?

   ☹ 1 2 3 4 5 6 ☺

High

Ease

B   A

C   B

Low

Low   Impact   High

A = Start today | B = This week
C = After all A & B

Notes

_____

_____

_____

_____

_____

_____

_____

_____

_____

_____

When Life Gives You Lemons, Make Lemonade

"Price is what you pay. Value is what you get." Warren Buffett

Handling the Seven Main Objections

Once you understand that there are seven categories objections can fall into, you will be able to foresee situations and respond to them more effectively. So say "goodbye" to the hot seat and "hello" to the benefits your newly developed problem-solving skills will attract. After you understand a buyer's objection, you will be able to handle it. However, how you handle it depends on the type of objection. Buyers object to many things in different ways, so knowing the seven categories an objection can fall into will make it easier to identify the most appropriate strategy to apply. Seven categories of objections:

1. Concealed objection

Concealed objections aren't always easy to identify. Physical movements, facial expressions, and the buyer's tone of voice can give you a clue about what they're thinking. Don't overestimate the power of listening; your ability to listen successfully will help you uncover a buyer's real objections. If a buyer doesn't know why they're hesitant to buy or if they're reluctant to discuss their concerns, questions are a great way to reveal their true objections.

2. Stalling objection

Stalling objections are fairly common in sales transactions. Your responsibility as a professional salesperson is to help the buyer analyse their reasons for and against buying and to determine if the objections they offer are true or just an excuse to get you out of the picture.

3. Not needed objection

This type of objection is often used by buyers to get rid of the salesperson without being rude. The irony is some salespeople actually facilitate this objection by presenting their product/service poorly.

4. Money objection

Money objections can be tricky because often the buyer will want to know the product's/service's price before the presentation, and they will not let you demonstrate how your product's/service's benefits outweigh its cost. If a buyer overreacts to your price, slow down the conversation. Listen to what they have to say and present your product's/service's benefits as they relate to cost.

5. Offer objection

Objections about the risks of purchasing an offer are more common than you may think. Buyers fear that what you're offering may not live up to your words or that it's not worth the time or money that they need to invest to use it. Also keep in mind that you're selling against the competition, so the buyer perhaps already has a competitive offer, has heard of one, or has used one in the past.

6. Supplier objection

This type of objection refers to the loyalty a buyer may have toward a supplier or salesperson. The buyer could also dislike you or your organisation. Often the best way to handle a supplier objection is to call the buyer frequently over a period of time. Get to know the buyer so that you can discover their needs and concerns.

7. Ethics

Sometimes buyers may require you to overcome situations that are unethical. Know you and your organisation's values well and follow them. Refer to your manager if in doubt.

TIP

A Word on Pricing
Offering the lowest price straight away will only lower your chances of sales success.

Self-Assessment
Rate Yourself on the Following:

1. How well do you understand the seven categories an objection can fall into?

    ☹   1   2   3   4   5   6   ☺

2. Rate your listening skills.

    ☹   1   2   3   4   5   6   ☺

3. What is your ability to determine if a buyer's objection is true or if they're trying to get rid of you?

    ☹   1   2   3   4   5   6   ☺

How urgently do you need to work on this?
Rank yourself below for both ease and impact.

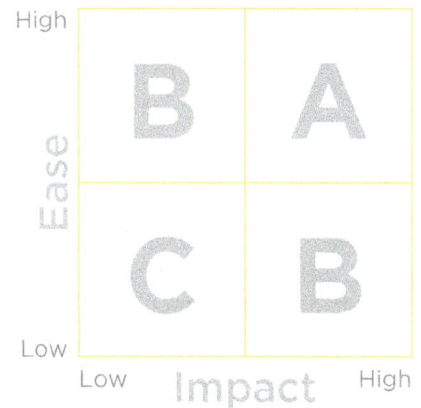

High		B	A
Ease			
		C	B
Low			
	Low	Impact	High

A = Start today | B = This week
C = After all A & B

Notes

_____

_____

_____

_____

The Closing Process

"I will persist until I succeed." Og Mandino

The Stages of the Closing Process

Sometimes salespeople have difficulties in closing. This can be easily avoided by gaining an understanding of how the closing process works. Follow this process to close like a pro:

The Start

1. Be enthusiastic
2. Visualise being successful
3. Confirm each of your clients' requirements
4. Expand each benefit to its requirement
5. Use pauses and do not rush

The Finish

1. Flesh out any objections
2. Use a trail close prior to handling each objection
3. Ask a final trail close
4. Ask for the business
5. Remain silent and wait for an answer wait for an answer.

Closing strategies

Once you have asked for a decision, remain silent. By keeping quiet for a few moments, you are maintaining the pressure on the client to make a decision. The silence shouldn't last longer than 30 seconds or so. If you keep quiet no matter how awkward this silence is, you will have a decision from them. Unless you are asking for a referral, once you have your client's order, finalise everything and finish the conversation as soon as is comfortably possible. In continuing to talk, you may say something inadvertently that changes your client's mind.

To be a successful salesperson, you must not be deterred if your client rejects you. If they say "no", determine their reasons and tackle them. You should attempt to close at least three times before you admit defeat. Up to five attempted closes should not offend your client, as long as these closes are well-executed. Attempting several closes in one sales call takes charm, personality, professionalism. If done well, it can result in a sale.

So, if your client dismisses your attempt at closing, try again. If they reject your close a second time, find out what the issue is, address it, and if appropriate, try to close again. If you still have no success, finish the conversation but agree on an actionable next step.

After the Close

The sale does not end with your client's signature on the dotted line. Commitment from them is merely one part of your business relationship them. It is the possibility of a future commitment which makes the sale a success. How you treat your client is the biggest factor in determining whether your client will do business with you again, so it is important that you do not lose interest immediately after securing commitment. After making the sale, you must follow up to be sure your product or service has been delivered when promised, set up correctly, and so on.

Following that, show your appreciation. Clients like to think that their business is appreciated, so it is important for you to show that you are grateful for the opportunity to work with them. A thank-you letter, perhaps with a small thank-you gift, will be enough to show them your gratitude without being intrusive, and it will increase the likelihood that they will do business with you in the future.

Self-Assessment
Rate Yourself on the Following:

How urgently do you need to work on this?
Rank yourself below for both ease and impact.

1. How well do you understand the closing process?

   ☹ 1   2   3   4   5   6   ☺

2. How often do you attempt closing?

   ☹ 1   2   3   4   5   6   ☺

3. How efficiently do you follow-up after a sale?

   ☹ 1   2   3   4   5   6   ☺

High

Ease

B   A

C   B

Low

Low   Impact   High

A = Start today | B = This week
C = After all A & B

Notes

_____

_____

_____

_____

_____

_____

_____

"Don't say I can't; say I won't."

Fritz Pearls

5. Active Listening

Desired result:

To have the client feel special and heard, and to easily gather the right information for a great presentation.

Active Listening Basics

"Words are, of course, the most powerful drug used by mankind." Rudyard Kipling

Active Listening Strategies

Active listening is a powerful sales tool. By really listening to your client (not just hearing them), and by convincing them that you are listening, you are demonstrating a genuine respect for them and their particular requirements.

Being a good listener is not inherent. It is not something you are born with. It is something you need to learn, and it is the result of hard work. It is one of the critical skills in selling, and it becomes especially important in telephone selling.

Benefits

1. By listening attentively to clients, you can develop a mutual understanding with them.

2. You will be able to confirm that you have really understood what your clients are saying, which will avoid any misunderstandings, and it will encourage them to feel more at ease.

3. Your clients will be more open and will say more as they feel that their comments are of value to you.

4. Actively listening is invaluable in building rapport between you and your client, for you will be able to fully appreciate exactly what it is that your client needs from you and make suggestions accordingly.

Pitfalls

1. Your attitude – boredom, frustration, elation, etc. – is much more obvious to people listening to you than it is to yourself, so keep your emotions in check.

2. Be aware that your client will sense when you are not listening, so ensure that you are focused at all times throughout the conversation. Now is not the time to check your emails!

Active Listening

1. Be genuinely interested in what the buyer has to say.

2. Make a hero of the buyer in the conversation rather than you.

3. Take great notes and use them to follow-up what is important to the buyer.

4. Hold back any judgement and suspend your frame of reference.

5. Don't jump in and never interrupt.

Self-Assessment
Rate Yourself on the Following:

How urgently do you need to work on this? Rank yourself below for both ease and impact.

1. How actively do you listen in general?

   ☹ 1   2   3   4   5   6   ☺

2. How well do you know your listening skills?

   ☹ 1   2   3   4   5   6   ☺

3. Rate your ability to take notes.

   ☹ 1   2   3   4   5   6   ☺

High

Ease

B   A

C   B

Low

Low   Impact   High

A = Start today | B = This week
C = After all A & B

Notes

_____

_____

_____

_____

_____

_____

_____

_____

_____

_____

Active Listening Techniques

"Lofty words cannot construct an alliance or maintain it; only concrete deeds do that." John F. Kennedy

Refine Your Skill

These four types of active listening techniques will help you develop your listening skills:

Technique	Reason	Action	Example
Encouraging	It's important to show your client that you are genuinely interested in what they have to say, and that you want them to continue talking.	Try not to agree or disagree with your client. Use non-committal words but with a positive tone of voice.	"I see" "OK" "Uh-huh"
Re-stating	Repeating what your client says shows that you are listening and really understand what their requirements are.	Reiterate your client's words but with your own comments.	"So if I've got this right, what you're saying is ..." "OK, so you're concerned that ..."
Empathising	By talking about your client's feelings, you are again demonstrating that you are listening and that you identify with them and their requirements.	Re-state your client's feelings.	"You feel that ..." "You were obviously upset that ..."
Summarising	Pulling together the important facts and ideas will keep you both on track and will establish the groundwork for future discussions.	Summarise the key points and ideas that have been discussed.	"So the main points you have made are ..." "OK, so it seems that your major requirement is that ..."

✓ Self-Assessment
Rate Yourself on the Following:

1. How well do you understand the four listening techniques?

   ☹ 1   2   3   4   5   6   ☺

2. How comfortable are you in using these techniques in your sales call?

   ☹ 1   2   3   4   5   6   ☺

3. How well do your clients respond to your active listening?

   ☹ 1   2   3   4   5   6   ☺

How urgently do you need to work on this?
Rank yourself below for both ease and impact.

High

Ease

B	A
C	B

Low

Low   Impact   High

A = Start today | B = This week
C = After all A & B

Notes

"Big people monopolise the listening; small people monopolise the talking."

David Schwartz

6. Building and Maintaining Rapport

Desired result:

To put the client in a comfortable state that is warm, receptive and friendly.

Rapport Basics

"If people around you will not hear you, fall down before them and beg their forgiveness, for in truth you are to blame." Fyodor Dostoyevsky

Effective Communication

Why Rapport?

Building rapport and maintaining it is a fundamental part of being an excellent salesperson. If you have rapport with your customers, they are more likely to listen to and communicate more effectively with you; you will interact more comfortably and they will trust you. Rapport is the very foundation for effective communication and positive relationship-building between you and your client.

Because of this, establishing rapport will dramatically increase your chances of winning a sale. People only buy from people they trust, so rapport must come before any kind of sale can take place.

Without rapport a sale is nearly impossible. Only when you notice that you are in rapport will you be able to begin to sell, and you must be invited by your client to sell. Your sale will only go ahead if your client has invited you to present your business to them. In order to get past the initial "hello" on the phone, you must quickly establish a relationship with them and develop enough rapport that they "invite" you to continue the process of presenting yourself and your business. Most sales opportunities fail because the salesperson has ignored the importance of establishing enough rapport so that an invitation is earned.

Also, without continued rapport, there will be no sale. Therefore, it is important to ensure that your rapport with your client is not broken.

> ## Key indicators that will tell you when you are in rapport with your clients are:
>
> 1. You will feel an openness between you.
>
> 2. You find yourself agreeing with each other.
>
> 3. Your client will be open to your suggestions even if they don't necessarily agree with you.

Self-Assessment
Rate Yourself on the Following:

1. How actively do you seek rapport in general?

   ☹ 1   2   3   4   5   6   ☺

2. How well do you know your rapport-building skills?

   ☹ 1   2   3   4   5   6   ☺

3. Rate your ability to build rapport.

   ☹ 1   2   3   4   5   6   ☺

How urgently do you need to work on this?
Rank yourself below for both ease and impact.

High		
	B	A
Ease		
	C	B
Low		
	Low	Impact	High

A = Start today | B = This week
C = After all A & B

Notes

_____

_____

_____

_____

_____

_____

_____

_____

_____

_____

Think About What You Say

"Success seems to be connected with action. Successful people keep moving. They make mistakes, but they don't quit." Conrad Hilton

Your Nonverbal Clues

As well as tuning in to your client's nonverbal signs, also be aware of the nonverbal clues that you transmit, as this affects how your client will read you.

Although you need to be natural in your conversation and you don't want to "ham it up", you will need to exaggerate your delivery to a certain extent. For example, by convey excitement or emotion to ensure that your client is interpreting you correctly. Clients cannot see your reactions through body language or facial expressions, so verbalise positive feelings. For example, your client can't see you smile, so ensure that they can hear your smile in your voice. Do this by laughing or making comments like "OK" with a smile on your face.

A well-delivered message will:

1. Sell an entire concept, not just a product or service.

2. Be heard by more people and with less words.

3. Create and maintain rapport.

Some tips to help you use your words well

1. Use action words and verbs. Action words and verbs will persuade your client's mind into action itself, thereby leading them into making a decision. If you can use words to get your client to think of the action that you want them to do, you are on your way to getting what you want.

2. Select the correct words so that you are selling, not telling. Telling and selling are two entirely different ideas. Telling imparts information whereas selling leads to an action. Telling focuses on the one doing the telling, whereas selling focuses on the receiver. Simply telling somebody something will not get you results.

3. People buy the outcome. Your client will not be won over purely by being presented the features and benefits of the product. They will need to see, feel, hear and understand the results. People will buy once they realise the benefits for themselves they will have as a direct result of the product/service. People want to know, "What's in it for me?"

4. Avoid "business talk". All too often, companies will use jargon and complicated, multi-syllabic words that they think will add credibility to their services. These words just confuse people or, worse, put them to sleep. So ensure that what you say is straightforward and easy to understand.

5. Change the way you say things, but not the concept itself. Maintain the integrity of what you're selling. The wrapping paper may be different, but the gift inside will remain the same.

There are a few traps to be wary of

1. What you say is not valuable enough to the client to be noticed.

2. What you say does not fit your client.

3. What you say does not include an action.

✓ Self-Assessment
Rate Yourself on the Following:

1. How well do you avoid the trap

   ☹ 1   2   3   4   5   6 ☺

2. How well do you use the tips?

   ☹ 1   2   3   4   5   6 ☺

3. How well can you regain your rapport?

   ☹ 1   2   3   4   5   6 ☺

How urgently do you need to work on this?
Rank yourself below for both ease and impact.

High	B	A
Ease	C	B
Low		

Low   Impact   High

A = Start today | B = This week
C = After all A & B

Notes

_____

_____

_____

_____

_____

_____

_____

_____

_____

_____

Positive Language Sells

"Every tomorrow has two handles. You can take the handle of worry or the handle of enthusiasm and more positive thought. As your choice goes, so will your day."
Anonymous

Words Matter
The Power of Words

Language is an extremely powerful tool. Whether you're communicating verbally or in writing, how you say things will affect whether your message is received positively or negatively. Although we all have the best intentions when it comes to communicating with our clients, we often say things in ways that can be interpreted as negative. Avoid falling into a negative language pattern by becoming aware of the implications of your words.

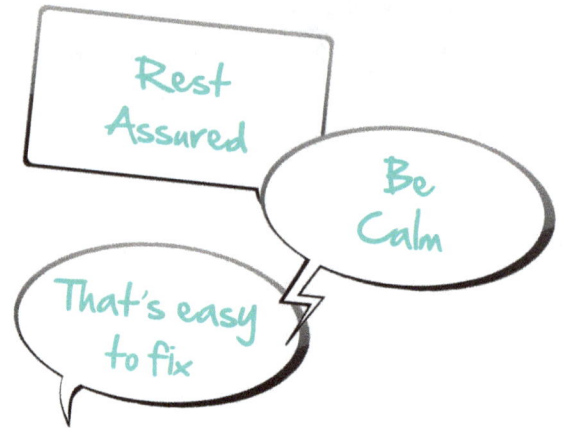

Rest Assured

Be Calm

That's easy to fix

Use the following examples as a guide:

Example	Client's Interpretation	Re-phrase
"No need to worry"	Worry	"Rest assured"
"It won't be difficult to fix"	Difficult	"That's easy to fix"
"Don't panic"	Panic	"Be calm"
"We're not expensive"	Expensive	"We're excellent value"

Self-Assessment
Rate Yourself on the Following:

1. How well do you understand the power of positive language?

   ☹   1   2   3   4   5   6   ☺

2. How aware are you of the "negative language" you are currently using in your presentations and proposals?

   ☹   1   2   3   4   5   6   ☺

3. How easily can you identify the difference between a negative attitude and using language that gives the impression of negativity?

   ☹   1   2   3   4   5   6   ☺

How urgently do you need to work on this?
Rank yourself below for both ease and impact.

High	B	A
Ease	C	B
Low		

Low   Impact   High

A = Start today | B = This week
C = After all A & B

Notes

_____

_____

_____

_____

_____

_____

_____

_____

_____

"Motivation is everything. You can do the work of two people, but you can't be two people. Instead, you have to inspire the next guy down the line and get him to inspire his people."

Lee Iacocca

7. Questioning

Desired result:

To have asked all the necessary questions, to maintain rapport, to gather the right information, and to build desire in the client.

Advanced Questioning Tips

"Be excited and enthusiastic about benefits!" Anonymous

Down the Right Road

1. Use benefits to create questions

Make sure you can get across benefits instead of features by creating a question sheet. Start with a benefit that your product/service helps soothe and then work backwards to create the question. Draw up a list of these benefits and practise them before you make your call so that you can build a strong desire in your client to take up your offer.

Example: Benefit: 24/7 online access.

Question: "Do you do your accounting work outside normal business hours?"

Response: "Yes"

Reply: "Would online access help you?"

2. Create building questions

You can take an existing problem such as "there is concern around safety" and build it by:

Making it bigger: "How often do you find that?

Showing where it came from: "Where are the biggest concerns?"

Linking it to other problems: "Does that also happen in other areas?"

3. Never present until you've asked enough questions

Make sure you have drilled down far enough to uncover sufficient client requirements to make a winning demonstration; otherwise, you will just be describing features instead of persuasive benefits.

4. Be professional and don't ask vague questions

Vague: "Does that happen often?"

Professional: "How often does that happen?"

Vague: "Do you think you will be able to do this?"

Professional: "When do you think you will be able to do this?"

Vague: "Do you have many x issues?"

Professional: "How many x issues do you have a year?"

5. Get examples

Client: "We are thinking about two options you suggested."

Salesperson: "Which is your favourite?"

6. Get agreement

"Let me see if I have this right ..."

"So if I am following you, you're saying that ..."

"It seems that what you want is ..."

7. Help the client identify issues

"If you had no constraints, what would you get?"

"How would you go about making that decision?"

"So what would be your main motivation for this?'

"What would you change about that if you could?"

"What is on your wish list?"

8. Use big-picture questions to develop needs

"How do you mean?'

"Like what?"

"And then what?"

"What else?"

9. Dare to ask the hard questions

"Is it fair to ask your opinion?"

"Mr. Buyer, are we at risk of not being able to do this?"

"If a 1 is 'no chance,' and a 5 is 'yes,' where would you say you are now?"

"Really, how much did you have in mind?"

✔ Self-Assessment
Rate Yourself on the Following:

How urgently do you need to work on this?
Rank yourself below for both ease and impact.

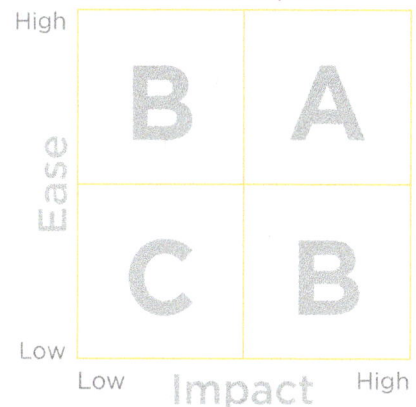

1. How well do you know the benefits of your product/service?

   ☹ 1 2 3 4 5 6 ☺

2. How confident do you feel asking hard questions?

   ☹ 1 2 3 4 5 6 ☺

3. How effective are you at drilling down and asking enough questions to uncover your prospect's requirements?

   ☹ 1 2 3 4 5 6 ☺

	Low Impact	High Impact
High Ease	B	A
Low Ease	C	B

Low — Impact — High

A = Start today | B = This week
C = After all A & B

"Do not let what you cannot do interfere with what you can do."

John Wooden

8. Planning

Desired result:

To give yourself the best chance of success, prepare for each call quickly, and take each call as far as it can go.

Advance the Sale

"Surprisingly, instead of an army of sensitive, soft-spoken top producers, many organisations have increasingly found themselves saddled with a generation of confused, hesitant, over trained, under-producing professional visitors." George W. Dudley and Dr F. Tanner, Jr., authors of "The Hard Truth About Soft-Selling: Restoring Pride & Purpose to the Sales Profession"

Moving Ahead

The sales process is a series of steps that the salesperson and the prospect must take together. We can call each step forward an "advance". Each contact without this is either a stall or a "no". A "no" is infinitely better than a stall, because you can make the decision to move on, or you will have an objection to overcome; either of these two means you can be proactive with your time and actions. However, a stall is an indefinite pause stuck in "no man's land".

Two Key Elements of an Advance

It must:

1. Have an activity or task that the **buyer** is carrying out, and

2. Be moving the sale forward.

By having the prospect actively carrying out a task, we can be sure that the prospect is involved in the process and the salesperson is being pro-active.

A great way to prepare an advance is the smart way:

S pecific
M easurable
A chievable
R elevant
T imeframe

Advances should be planned prior to each sales contact. They will set the agenda and ensure that your contacts are much more than a professional visit.

TIP **Planning Advances**
You should set two advances for each and every contact without exception, and you should prepare for both of them. The first advance and your main goal is a realistic stretch that makes you aim for something that will test you, and the second is a fallback that you can achieve even if the contact goes very poorly. In this way every single contact you have will be moving the sale closer.

Examples of an Advance

An advance:

1. Prospect is assessing your offer.

2. Prospect is arranging a referral.

3. Prospect is collecting information for you.

Not an advance:

1. You are to call back.

2. The prospect agrees to a contact sometime in the future.

3. The prospect will be in touch if things change.

Reporting

The extent and frequency of advances can be discussed at sales meetings so that valuable time is spent on what is moving the sale forward, what needs to be done to move it forward, and how these can be shared amongst the team.

In addition, your Customer Relationship Management system (CRM) should allow the easy entry and analysis of advances for every contact, in particular outlining the last advance and the next advance. If a record does not show an advance, then the prospect and the sale is stalled, and this needs to be rectified.

Self-Assessment
Rate Yourself on the Following:

How urgently do you need to work on this?
Rank yourself below for both ease and impact.

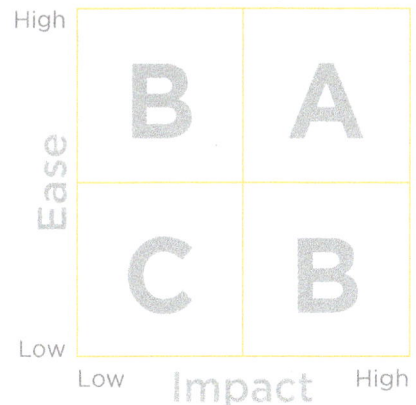

1. How well do you end with an advance?

    ☹ 1 2 3 4 5 6 ☺

2. How well do you plan your advances prior to each contact?

    ☹ 1 2 3 4 5 6 ☺

3. How well do you seek additional advances during the one contact?

    ☹ 1 2 3 4 5 6 ☺

	High		
Ease	B	A	
	C	B	
Low			
	Low	Impact	High

A = Start today | B = This week
C = After all A & B

Notes

"Look at a day when you are supremely satisfied at the end. It's not a day when you lounge around doing nothing; it's when you had everything to do, and you've done it."

Margaret Thatcher

9. Up-selling and Cross-selling

Desired result:

To engage with a buying customer and open up potential opportunities for them to make further purchases.

Selling Doesn't Stop with the Sale

"Don't find customers for your products; find products for your customers." Seth Godin

Selling needn't stop when the buying process begins, yet many salespeople overlook this opportunity to continue to sell their product, and in doing so miss out on a rich avenue for profit generation.

Cross-selling and up-selling are both sales techniques that occur when the purchase is already in progress. Both are intended to increase the value to the buyer and the seller.

Since selling is getting the right message to the right person at the right time, what better time to sell than when the customer is in the process of buying from you.

Contrary to some salespeople's fears, most customers actually appreciate being informed about the additional products that might better meet their needs or something that has just become available.

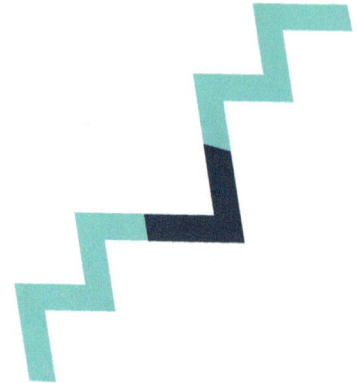

Cross-selling

When a company has multiple products related to their main product line it provides the opportunity for you, the salesperson to offer complementary products or services. So cross-selling occurs when you help the customer to purchase something additional to what they originally intended to purchase.

For example, someone comes into a bank wanting to open an account and the account manager discovers they haven't stared a retirement investment account and sells them on the benefits of doing that.

Up-selling

The aim of up-selling on the other hand is to paint a picture for the customer that helps them see the benefits of purchasing a higher end version of the same product.

For example, your customer may be interested in purchasing a basic life insurance policy and is shown by the seller how for just a few dollars more a month they can have a number of additional benefits.

Different applications

When cross-selling, your job is to identify an additional need the customer has and sell them the product that will meet that need in addition to what they are already purchasing.

Upselling is less needs based and more about building value in the product and explaining the benefits of that higher value product.

Tips for using these techniques

1. Make sure you are fully informed about all the products your company sells

2. Introduce additional information at key points in the sales conversation for example:

    a. After a trial close

    b. After a request for more information

    c. After making a strong selling point

    d. When you've successfully closed

    e. When you have earned the clients trust

Only recommend products or services your customer can truly use. There is no long term merit in selling someone something they don't need, and it could damage your reputation.

Self-Assessment
Rate Yourself on the Following:

How urgently do you need to work on this?
Rank yourself below for both ease and impact.

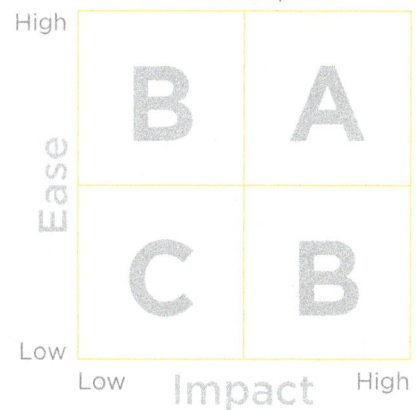

1. I use comprehensive knowledge of products to upsell and increase my revenue.

    ☹   1   2   3   4   5   6   ☺

2. I understand when to use up-selling and when to use cross-selling techniques.

    ☹   1   2   3   4   5   6   ☺

3. I always try to determine what other products might be useful for my client.

    ☹   1   2   3   4   5   6   ☺

High

Ease

B   A

C   B

Low

Low   Impact   High

A = Start today | B = This week
C = After all A & B

Notes

_____

_____

_____

_____

_____

Cross-selling and Up-selling Techniques

"If you always do what you've always done, you'll always get what you always got."
Alison Morris

You as a salesperson need to become completely familiar with the techniques for cross-selling and up-selling; when to use one or the other and when to employ both. You also need to know when not to use these techniques.

When not to use cross-selling and up-selling

When you have not deliberately chosen and correctly positioned either your add-on or upsell so that it will add value for your customer, you should consider how that customer will perceive your actions.

Remember, the average customer is quite savy when a salesperson uses these techniques clumsily and they will likely find your suggestions irrelevant and annoying. However, the following should also all be considered when evaluating what you are trying to accomplish.

1. When trying to modify a sale you must be sure the cross-sell won't jeopardise the original sale.

2. A cross-sell will either increase or decrease your profit margin depending on the cost of the additional product purchased. If your current goal is to increase your profit margins then you want to make sure the additional product you recommend has higher margins than the original purchase.

3. If however your strategy is to increase growth then you may be willing to sacrifice profitability and focus on increasing conversions.

4. A successful up-sell results in an increase in revenue and hopefully an increase in profit margins as well.

5. However, if you come across as pushy or unconvincing the customer will likely refuse.

Putting the techniques to use

1. Have your client's best interests at heart. If you don't think your client can sense this, you're wrong.

2. Adopt the role of valued advisor.

3. Understand how the client thinks and what is important to them in order to build motivation.

4. Carefully chose the best products based on an understanding of the clients world.

5. Practice makes perfect.

Learn from Companies who do it right!

The most successful companies have a conversion rate of 33%. Where they differ from other companies is in their customer retention rates which can be as high as 95%. Here's what they have learned and practice:

1. It's easier to cultivate current clients than find new ones
2. Introducing existing customers to new products and services works
3. Existing customers yield higher profitability
4. Satisfied current customers frequently refer others
5. Reframe cross-selling and up-selling as "additional services"
6. Make suggestions based on the individual customer's preferences. For example, you liked this before so we suggest you look at this product now. It makes the customer feel special.

TIP

1. **Look for opportunities amongst your existing customers**
2. **Make sure they are aware of new products and special offers.**

Self-Assessment
Rate Yourself on the Following:

How urgently do you need to work on this?
Rank yourself below for both ease and impact.

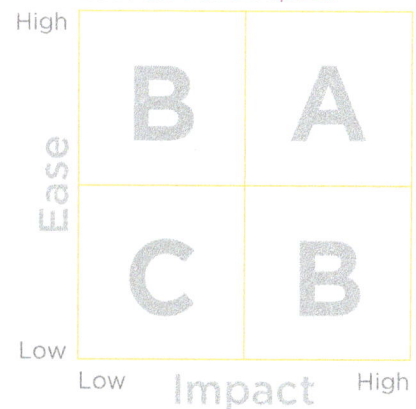

1. I take every available opportunity to cross-sell and up-sell.

   ☹ 1 2 3 4 5 6 ☺

2. I analyse my existing customer base for additional sales opportunities.

   ☹ 1 2 3 4 5 6 ☺

3. I always try to understand the customer's needs prior to suggesting an up-sell or cross-sell

   ☹ 1 2 3 4 5 6 ☺

	High	
	B	A
Ease	C	B
	Low	

Low   Impact   High

A = Start today | B = This week
C = After all A & B

Notes

_____

_____

_____

Improving Conversion Rates

"Change before you have to." Jack Welch

Conversion rates are defined as the percentage of customers you have contact with who make a purchase.

Products with lower price points tend to have higher conversion rates, while products with higher price points, because of the additional involvement of the customer, will generally have lower conversion rates.

Improving your conversion rates is the best way to increase your sales and profits. In fact, most companies generate all the leads they need. The problem comes in not being able to convert them.

So right from the beginning of the call you should be generating ideas for an upcoming cross-sell or up-sell opprotunities.

Tips for using the cross-sell and the up-sell to increase conversion rates

The Up-sell:

1. Assume the customer wants it. Up-selling can be practically effortless. The customer has already gone ahead with a major purchase. You can present the up-sell in a "by-the-way manner" and briefly explain a major benefit.

2. Use the indecision. If your customer isn't sure exactly what product they want, it's a great time to up-sell by offering guidance and suggestions.

3. Be specific about what you're suggesting and be enthusiastic. The customer needs to know you think the product is fantastic.

The Cross-sell:

1. Sell the value. Make sure your customer sees the value for them in the cross-sell while at the same time letting them know you appreciate their business.

2. Show savings. If there is a savings attached to bundling more than one product or buying a second item let the customer know this up front.

3. Stay relevant with your suggestions. Don't overload the customer with too many choices. They are likely to decline all of them.

4. Offer a range of prices. For example, you might suggest 3 differently priced add-ons for the customer to consider, all with unique benefits and at varying price points.

Tips for using these techniques

1. For new leads: Make sure you qualify your leads right up front. You can do this by offering a specific proposition to those who aren't ready, can't pay or have no interest in your product, leaving you with leads who have the motivation, desire and capacity for the product. Now you have the time to concentrate on the high quality leads.

2. Look in the right places. Successful companies talk to customers who are already familiar with their product, already use it or have a high probability of using it. Don't waste time trying to convince someone who isn't interested.

3. Get to the essence of the customers problem or needs. You can't sell a solution without knowing what it is.

4. Help your customers understand the compelling reasons why they should take action. What are the values and benefits to them? What do they stand to lose by not moving forward?

5. Continually train to increase your sales skills. Understand how to use strategic, non-manipulative selling principles.

6. Use the telephone as a powerful business tool by recognising it may be the only contact the customer has with your company. Make sure your skills are impeccable and you always leave a great impression.

7. Persist with constant follow ups. 80% of all significant sales occur after the fifth follow up. You will beat the competition by hanging in for the follow up as only about 8% of salespeople make it to that fifth call.

Self-Assessment
Rate Yourself on the Following:

How urgently do you need to work on this?
Rank yourself below for both ease and impact.

1. I am consist with my cross-selling and up-selling efforts. I use them in each and every sales transaction.

   ☹ 1   2   3   4   5   6 ☺

2. I target high quality customers to increase my conversion rates.

   ☹ 1   2   3   4   5   6 ☺

3. I have targets and goals for myself for improving my techniques and conversion rate.

   ☹ 1   2   3   4   5   6 ☺

High

Ease

B   A

C   B

Low

Low   Impact   High

A = Start today | B = This week
C = After all A & B

Notes

Additional Cross-selling and Up-selling Opportunities

"If you work just for money, you'll never make it. But if you love what you are doing, and always put the customer first, success will be yours." Ray Kroc

In this chapter there has been an emphasis on the hidden revenue in cross-selling and up-selling. Especially as it can cost 4 times as much to sell to a new customer as an existing one. However, these opportunities often aren't acted on because of fear of risking the sale by "asking for more".

You can eliminate that fear by gathering in-depth information about your customers and prospects to uncover hidden sales opportunities.

Tips for thinking like your customer

1. Realise that your customer does NOT think like you. This is a classic mistake salespeople make. They think the customer likes and wants the product for the same reasons they would. Keep an open mind. Let the customer tell you what they think.

2. Adapt to the way the customer is behaving rather than wishing they would behave like you would.

3. Don't lead with the product. This short circuits any opportunity to probe for what the customer needs, and wants to accomplish.

4. Remember, that while you know the product well, the customer often doesn't. When you lead with features and benefits, the customer doesn't know whether or not that feature or benefit is relevant to them.

5. When discussing the product use real life situations that your customer can relate to.

Evaluating current customer needs

1. Customers often don't know exactly what their problems are. Listen to what they are saying. Are they complaining about something? Are they longing for something they wish they had? Be a detective.

2. In general, people want one of 6 needs satisfied when they buy. Which one does your customer want satisfied?
   - To make things easier
   - Physical comfort
   - Mental stimulation
   - Peace of mind
   - Identity reinforcement
   - Social acknowledgment

3. Don't fall in to the trap of just listening for problems that fit what you offer.

The right time to cross-sell and up-sell

1. The right time to begin using these techniques is before you even speak with the customer.

2. For efficiency, make a list of your top customers and note what they have bought from you. This should uncover opportunities to offer more solutions the customer hasn't purchased yet.

3. If you have done your homework, that is, identifying the trends, needs and issues that are important to your customer, then you can continually be looking for ways to get the most out of every contact.

4. This doesn't mean selling your customer something they don't need but more of something they do need.

Self-Assessment
Rate Yourself on the Following:

How urgently do you need to work on this?
Rank yourself below for both ease and impact.

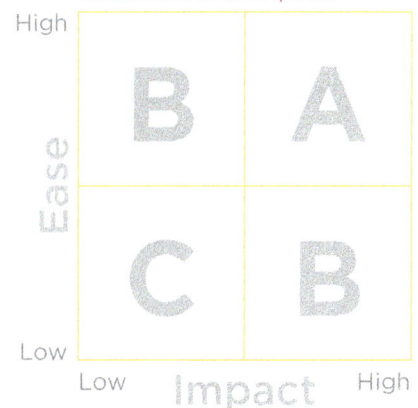

1. I know how to prepare ahead of time for cross-sell and up-sell opportunities.

    ☹ 1   2   3   4   5   6   ☺

2. I try to find out what underlying general need my customers have.

    ☹ 1   2   3   4   5   6   ☺

3. I use real life situations to help my customers understand my product.

    ☹ 1   2   3   4   5   6   ☺

4. I always begin my sale by finding out more about my customer so I can provide relevant solutions.

    ☹ 1   2   3   4   5   6   ☺

High

Ease

B	A
C	B

Low

Low   Impact   High

A = Start today | B = This week
C = After all A & B

Notes

_____

_____

_____

_____

Putting it all together: What to Say to Customers

"The great aim of education is not knowledge, but action." Herbert Spencer

This chapter has emphasised the need to pre-plan for your telephone exchanges. This means having superior knowledge of your products, and if you are contacting existing clients, knowing what they have purchased and their history with your company.

Much of how you respond during the actual call will be based on the responses you get from your client; however you will always be probing for more information and looking for opportunities to provide the client with additional services. Don't follow a script – nothing turns off clients more than a salesperson who sounds like they are reading from a cookie cutter script.

Use these examples to create your own

1. "George, many of my clients are also taking advantage of ... because ..." (Beginning the cross-sell)

2. "That's an excellent choice. I should tell you also we're running a special offer right now. If you purchase contents insurance we will decrease your premium by 10%. You'll also get the first year of a visa card free." (The up-sell)

3. "Mary, I think you've picked an excellent policy. The smart way to go for just $100 more a year is to increase your coverage to 2 million dollars, which is what ABC is now recommending. That would be your best move on this ..." (The up-sell)

4. "Frank, I know your trip to Canada is coming up quickly. I recommend you also sign up for our credit card because it covers you for trip cancellation, lost baggage and travel insurance, all of which would cost you extra if you had to pay for them separately." (The cross-sell, after customers have bought travellers cheques)

5. "Susan, since your parents are co-signing the loan with you, I would highly recommend you take out our loan insurance. If anything were to happen to you, it would put your parents into financial hardship to pay off the loan and I'm sure you don't want that." (The cross-sell)

6. "Jim, I would suggest you add earthquake insurance to your home insurance package. It's something most people don't think to do, but with your home sitting in a high risk area you could sustain devastating loses without it." (The cross-sell)

7. "Carol you've been with the bank now for 10 years as a loyal client. We have just introduced a new program for our best clients you will be interested in hearing about. When you let us invest $100,000 with our wealth management services, you get a number of special benefits including your own personal account manager, preferential treatment on mortgage rates and lines of credit, priority banking and access to our worldwide business centres. I know you travel for business frequently. We are available to you 24 hours a day, 7 days a week to help from anywhere in the world." (The up-sell)

8. "Simon, it's an excellent idea to have personal life insurance so that Mary and the kids are covered should anything happen to you. For a few dollars more you would be wise to have a policy on Mary. Let me explain what that would look like." (The cross-sell)

These are just some of the kinds of statements you can make once you have determined client need. Remember: **Practice. Practice. Practice.**

TIP **Always assume the sale and always believe you are selling the best product for your client.**

✔ Self-Assessment
Rate Yourself on the Following:

How urgently do you need to work on this? Rank yourself below for both ease and impact.

1. I always prepare ahead of time for a call with an existing client.

☹   1   2   3   4   5   6   ☺

2. I write my own dialogues so that they sound natural.

☹   1   2   3   4   5   6   ☺

3. I take notes during the call so I can keep track of client needs.

☹   1   2   3   4   5   6   ☺

High

Ease

Low

B	A
C	B

Low   Impact   High

A = Start today | B = This week
C = After all A & B

Notes

_____

_____

_____

_____

_____

_____

_____

_____

_____

Congratulations!

Congratulations on finishing this important sales training. While a career in sales may come easier to some people than others, there is no such thing as a "natural born salesperson." Every person you consider to be successful in sales has had to work at their craft by applying lessons like the ones found in this book.

Now that you've completed this book, go back through the pages and circle the three or four lessons you most need to work on. Then return to this book monthly to make sure you are reinforcing the lessons learned and refining your skill. Though sales is not for the faint of heart, it is a perfect job for those ready to work with all their heart. Apply the lessons you've learned through this course and find yourself more effective.

In the end, a career in sales is not about accumulating wealth. Rather, a successful career in sales will provide you a great sense of accomplishment as you align the solutions you possess with the needs of others. You will have the pleasure of earning a living while knowing that you are instrumental in solving the problems and meeting the needs of many.

It's my hope that you take the skills learned in this course to benefit others, and that as you do you will generate more opportunites, greater income, and deeper professional fulfillment.

Ready for More?

The contents of this book and many more sales lessons are available as virtual workshops online at the Accela Learning Centre. Here you can instantly access additional training and work towards graduating with an Accela certificate. Turbo charge your career by visiting www.accela.com.au for more information.

Index

Notes

Notes

www.ingramcontent.com/pod-product-compliance
Lightning Source LLC
Chambersburg PA
CBHW061105210326
41597CB00021B/3984